Making Party Food

Photography by Bill Thomas

A strawberry milk drink

You will need:

strawberries

yoghurt

honey

milk

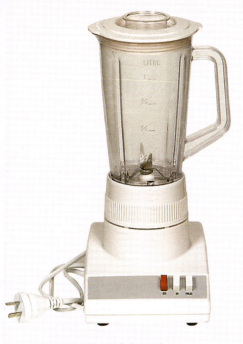

blender

Mum or Dad

can turn the blender on and off for you.

Cut up
the strawberries.

Put them into the blender

with one cup

of cold milk.

Ask Mum to turn the blender on.
The strawberries
and the milk
will go round
and round.

When they are mixed together,
ask Mum to turn the blender off.

Put the strawberry yoghurt
and some honey into the blender.

Ask Mum to turn the blender
on and off again.

Now your strawberry milk drink
is ready.

A banana boat

You will need:

banana   ice cream   biscuits   popcorn

Take the skin
off the banana.

Make a long cut
in the banana.

Open the banana
just a little bit.

Put some ice cream
in the bowl.

Put the banana
on the ice cream.

Put more ice cream
inside the banana.

Push the biscuits
into the ice cream.
Now your banana
looks like a boat.

Put the popcorn
in the bowl.
The popcorn
will look like waves around the boat.

A fruit hedgehog

You will need:

orange

lots of fruit like this.

toothpicks

Ask Mum or Dad
to cut the orange
for you.

Make the eyes
and the nose
for the hedgehog
with fruit.

Cut up the fruit
into little bits.

Put the fruit
on the toothpicks.

Push the toothpicks into the orange.
Now you have made
a fruit hedgehog.

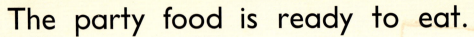

The party food is ready to eat.